HONOR YOUR INNER TREASURES
FINDING FULFILLMENT AND HAPPINESS through HARMONY OF MIND AND SPIRIT

CELINA TIO & RAYMOND AARON

ISBN: 978-1-77277-085-8

PUBLISHED BY:
10-10-10 PUBLISHING
MARKHAM, ON
CANADA

Disclaimer:

The information contained in this book is intended to be educational and motivational.
The information contained in this book should not replace consultation with a competent healthcare professional.
The author and publisher are in no way liable for any misuse of the material.

Contents

Dedication & Appreciation

This book is dedicated with deepest gratitude and infinite love to my husband Diego Ferreyra, for his unconditional love and support, for sharing and co-creating with me our life's journey.

Special thanks to:

- Nina for her unconditional love and for bringing into our lives her natural loving wisdom.
- Raymond Aaron, for gratefully opening a door in my life. Co-authoring this book with Raymond fills my heart with appreciation and gratitude. Thank you Raymond for believing in me, professionally and personally, for your generosity, inspiration and brilliant teachings.
- Wai-Lin Terry for her magnificent support in the creation of this book, and Lisa Browning for adding her professional spark in editing this book.
- Lori Murphy and Jennifer Le from the Raymond Aaron Group, for their professional input and guidance.
- My family - my mother ……, who lives in my heart, Aurora Olga, my father Tomas and sisters Silvana, Marisa and Vanesa, my cousin Lorena, aunt Pili and uncle Rogelio. My nephews and nieces. Thank you for always being there for me.
- Special people in my life - Monica Bertilotti and Dr. Julio C. Duran for their love, support, friendship and inspiration.
- Every person who has come into my life and shared light, love for life, teachings and inspiration and for opening their lives to me.

A blessing to you:

- Because deep inside you know that you are here to shine, to be successful, happy, healthy and to enjoy and thrive in your life. YOU are the reason for your own life and I encourage you to live unhesitatingly in your true power.

Testimonials

"This book takes you into a journey of inner discovery, guiding you to the most powerful being you will ever meet. Your true self!"
Mark McKoy, Olympic Champion, 110mH. 1992, Barcelona

"Reading this book is an incredible touching and beautiful journey. I not only feel empowered but also connected."
Can Zheng, Award Winning Author of "Empower Chinese"

"There is great power, infinite abundance, unlimited resources and genuine love in you. This book motivates you to tap into your unique Inner Treasures and live your life fully."
Francis Ablola, Marketing Authority and Award Winning Advertising Writer

Foreword

Are you ready to recreate yourself? Celina Tio knows that you have inner treasures, yet you tend to be dismissive of yourself, your desires, and your needs. Sometimes you are overpowered by the weight of the world. All too often you are unaware of who you really are or who you want to be; therefore, ignoring your potential along the way. In Honor Your Inner Treasures, Celina Tio and Raymond Aaron take you on a journey to re-discover yourself. You will learn how to let go of your past in order to find your authentic self. You will learn how to let go of fear to embrace change. Once you have transformed yourself into the person you want to be, you will discover a wealth of potential!

Would you like to be as powerful as you want to be? Are you ready to take advantage of what you have inside? You will discover how you can do these things when you read Honor Your Inner Treasures. Celina Tio shares how to access your inner power by tuning in to your body, mind, and spirit. Once you become aware of the amazing potential within you, she shares how to harness that internal power. Celina would love to sit down with each of you to help you connect directly with your inner being. She will help you discover and honor your unique inner treasures through the Honor Your Inner Treasures™ Program.

Loral Langemeier
The Millionaire Maker

Introduction

Know me by my blessings, not my sorrows.
-Celina Tio

Some people write because they have a story to tell. Others write because they need to make themselves heard. When Raymond and I write, however, we realize deeply that this is simply the medium we have chosen to reach out to you.

From my end, I am writing this book because I see you, and I see your sorrows. This is terrible to me, because I can also so clearly see the beauty that is as much a part of you as your heart, your skin and your bones. Why should such beauty be laden with sorrow, and how could I ever turn away and not offer you my hand?

I see you.

I see you sitting on the bus with your shoulders hunched up around your ears, trying to crawl away from the world. Your breath is stuttered and harsh, and I want to touch you gently, showing you how to inhale life and how to exhale peace.

I hear you, too! I'll bet that sometimes I hear you when you wish that no one would, but underneath that, I hear someone who yearns to be heard. Sometimes you whisper about how broken you are, or how unlucky life has left you.

I can touch your frown with my fingers, and I can read the story of your life spinning around you like a large whirling cloud. There are things that lash at you, and try to hold you back, but right now, my dear, I know something that you do not.

I know that you are a wonderful person, and I know how smart and strong you are. The great Creator has gifted you, the way that every other being on this planet has been gifted, and those gifts are amazing. If I sat next to you, I could feel that strength vibrating through your frame, creating a thrum that could quell mountains and stop rivers. In your pure form, you are mighty, and you are eternal.

It's hard to feel mighty and eternal some days, though, isn't it? We are made from the same materials that were kindled in the heart of dying stars, and we see farther and deeper than anything else in the world, but that still doesn't spare us the pain that the world brings.

We are still affected by things like abuse, divorce, poverty, pain and malice. We have the vulnerability to be hurt, so deeply and so violently that it is a wonder we are still standing. Sometimes, in the middle of a world that feels like it is doing its level best to destroy us, we forget how immortal we are and how perfect. We reach for the simplest and crudest tools that are available to us instead of searching out the talents that reside within.

Raymond and I are the last people in the world to tell you that you should not be in pain. The world can be a hurtful place, with as much ferocity as it is joyous, and sometimes it seems that the people who we love the most, the ones who we treasure and cherish, are the first ones to leave us.

Sometimes it feels as if it's not gravity that makes the world run, but pain. However, just as we were given pain, we were given the gifts to deal with it. Your gifts are luminous. They outnumber the stars in the sky, and I want to help you find them.

Because we live in a world where our gifts are not recognized, celebrated or treasured, we bury them and chase other things instead. We think about wealth when we should be thinking about love, we think about fun toys when we should be thinking about nourishing ourselves.

I want to direct your attention back to yourself. Look inside yourself in the right way, and soon enough, you will see treasures that could make a king weep in jealousy. These treasures are unique to you, and no one can do the things you do, or see the things that you see.

Sometimes, the beauty of the people around me hurts me because it is so very sharp. There is an escalation and upleveling in energy that comes from seeing the potential that floats all around me, and then there is a deep and abyssal pain because some of my nearest and dearest never recognize the real gifts and the real power that they have.

Because I spent so many years hiding from my own light, I know exactly what that is like, and I know how powerful the pull of that darkness is. I know exactly how hard it can be to pull yourself from the darkness, but I did it. It was difficult at first, because I was fighting an entire life's worth of training and pain. For a while, it felt like the entire world was trying to force me back, but once I had taken those first few steps, I realized how light I was feeling.

It wasn't long before I realized that my strengths were such that they could repel any darkness, fight back any grief or any challenge. I was only struggling because the world was weighing me down. The pressures that came from outside of myself were no match for the beauty that was inside me.

I spend my life now sharing what I have within. I make sure that people know how special they are. I show them the strength that they truly have inside them, and I help them figure out where they can go with it. One of my gifts is showing other people theirs, and that's what I want, more than anything to do for you right now.

If your life has made you dark, and made you sad, if you are grieving, and if you are in pain, take my hand, and let me show you how to heal yourself. There is power in you that you've never seen before, and I will show you how to use it!

Before your journey into this book co-authored with Raymond Aaron, I would like to share this poem that I penned especially for you.

Imagine for a moment that you are a pure, perfect, brilliant diamond laying on the palm of the hand of an appraiser.
Now imagine that the appraiser is the creator of the universe.
Your creator!

Close your eyes and allow your heart to expand...
Can you feel how purely loved you are?
Can you sense your perfection?
Can you see your brilliance?
Embrace and accept your true nature
because you are all you want to become.

Honor Your Inner Treasures

Open your eyes now and allow your heart to expand even more
and start living your dream life.
You are already blessed!

Celina Tio, January 2015

Chapter 1
Collectively Created Me

Small as a seed that grew to be
More than extraordinary,
my life was transformed.
- Celina Tio

We come into this world so trusting, innocent and full of life. Even as babies, we are amazingly unique, and even at that tender age, we are powerful. We want to live, we want to laugh, and we want to experience everything that the world has to offer us.

However, one important thing to remember is that from the moment a baby takes its first breath, it is being influenced by the people around it. There is never a moment when we are not touched in some way by the people and the events that surround us, but instead of making us less unique, it only makes us more beautiful!

What Touches Us?

There are so many things that inform who we are. Some people laugh and tell me that they are true, pure individuals. While I do not disagree with them, I count up the influences that make up what they are in my head. School, work, lost first loves, parental discord, death. Absolutely no one goes through life without being touched by the world, and instead of fighting it, you need to embrace it!

Our families shape us. Whether you are raised by your natural or adoptive family, they shape the way you look, the way you react, the way you enjoy things and the things we dislike.

We are all born into a certain body. Some of us are tall, others are thin, still others feel that their bodies are entirely wrong from bottom to top. Our bodies affect how we move, and how we experience the world.

Our religion and our culture shape us in obvious ways, but our standing in the hierarchy of siblings shapes us in more subtle ways.

Exams at school tell us what we're good at, while bullies tell us that we cannot be good at anything at all.

Finally, there's the ever present media that reminds us that we are not good enough, not smart enough, not pretty enough, and only worthy of love if we fit into a very narrow category of human being. Even then, we are only worth time and effort if we have the money to put into it.

Understanding the Ego

Everything that affects and touches us is solidified into layers that cover our tender inner hearts, like a mask. Somewhere underneath that layer is the real you, but for anything in the world to get to you, it has to go through the protective layer first, and vice versa.

These layers are known as your ego. People say that the ego is a bad thing, but the truth is that it helps us function in society. It is the part of us that forms our personality, and it is very important. You cannot separate yourself from your ego, and honestly, you should not try. When you lop off bits of yourself, you are only going to end up bitter and hurt in so many ways. I don't like it when people I know try to cut off the bits of themselves that they find objectionable. It hurts them, and it hurts me!

Instead of fighting your ego, you need to sit down with it and learn from it. This process can be long, and it is always full of surprises. Some of these surprises are good, but some of them can be quite terrible.

For example, a little while ago, I was helping a friend who hated dogs. Now, my friend is a lovely woman. She is kind and sweet and gentle, but when she sees a dog, even if it is a darling little thing, she curls her lip and looks away.

I finally asked her one day why she did this. Why did she express such disgust over something that was so cute and harmless? Had she ever been bit? She said no. I asked her if she was allergic, and she said no. The more I asked her, the more confused and upset she looked, and finally, she confessed that she had no idea why she disliked dogs so much.

I caught up with my friend later, and she rushed to tell me what she had learned. Essentially, it seemed that her step-mother had a little dog. The dog was perfectly sweet-natured, but because my friend did not get along with her step-mother, those feelings were transferred first to that dog, and then to all dogs.

Upon realizing how much of her life had been affected by her step-mother, my friend was aghast. She had not realized that she carried that weight of anger with her. She thought she was free of it, and that her step-mother could not affect her any more. Despite the fact that she was a grown woman, however, her step-mother's reach still landed on her!

I talked with my friend, and together we identified what was hurting her, and what parts were remnants of having been influenced by a woman she thought of as cruel and hurtful. My friend has recovered, and she is doing quite well these days.

One of the real signs of success, I think, is that she recently adopted a puppy from the local humane shelter!

Admitting To Our Layers

Sometimes, we do not want to talk about the things that affected us. Sometimes the things that affect us to this day are terrible and it causes us pain just to think about them. In some cases, the experiences were so bad that our bodies and our minds have shut down to the fact that they did take place.

However, if you are going to truly come into your full strength, you must look at the layers of your ego and name them. Is one of your layers abuse? Is another one a disease? What about the layer created by school yard bullies? These are all things that are going to affect the way that you move forward, and the way that you show your strength.

Do not be afraid of the experiences, the situations and the emotions that have made you what you are. If you were hurt by something and you feel ashamed of it, it is past time to let that shame go. You are not at fault for things that happened to you. Whether you could defend yourself or not, you are not the one to blame for other people's evil.

Sometimes, the layers of our ego are in place to cover mistakes that we have made. Many years ago, I met a man who was very depressed. He could not hold down a job, he struggled with substance abuse, and he was cruel to the people around him. I spoke to him, and as the conversation stretched further and further, there was a single thought that occurred to me.

"What is it?" I asked quietly. "What can you not forgive yourself for?"

He never told me, but his eyes filled up with tears and he averted my gaze. I waited for a long moment, and when he did not look up again, I walked away, grief in my heart.

This was a man who at least felt he had done terrible things, and he allowed his grief and his guilt over whatever it was to warp his life.

It can help to think about the layers of our ego as being variously translucent or opaque. A good layer allows us to see clearly and it allows our light to shine clearly through. This is a good layer as it can even intensify the light.

A bad layer is one that is murky and opaque. Instead of letting our light reach the world, it blocks it. It might even distort the light so that we are putting something dark and disturbing out instead.

Then there are layers that are somewhere in between. These layers bend the light or color it, but this is not necessarily a bad thing. Many artists have layers to their ego that bend things just right. This allows them to have a certain kind of vision that is denied to other people, and they may have to be patient enough to wait for the public to catch up to them.

A Call to Action

Today, as you read these very words, I am calling on you to take action. You now know what an ego is, and you know how it is created. What I want you to do is to sit down and learn more about your ego.

This exercise is so simple, but so effective. Take a piece of paper and using a pencil, write down something that you know created a layer of your ego. It might be something as big as your parents, or it might be something as small as a compliment someone paid you years ago.

Now write down everything that you think resulted from it. If someone paid you a compliment on a certain dress, you might have developed a fondness for that color. If your parents were over-protective, you might never have learned to take care of yourself.

When you are done, look at the list. What do you think that layer is like? Is it clear? Is it murky? Is it beautiful in its own right?

We are all created from our experiences, and the first step towards embracing our inner treasures is to acknowledge this.

You are wonderful, and the experiences that took you to this point are all part of that journey. Do not be afraid of yourself; instead, let yourself shine!

Chapter 2
I Am No One

I used to think I had a lot of problems to solve.
Now I know I have a lot of things to learn.
- Celina Tio

There is the panic and desperation that comes when things are in motion and when they are moving fast. When times like that rise up like a red, red tide, they are terrifying, but you know that you need to stay afloat. You need to fight, you need to struggle, and even if there is no end in sight, you know what you need to do.

We describe these times as being terrifying and fraught but, for many people, the periods of quiet are even worse. When things get quiet, you are left alone with your thoughts, and instead of being full and content, you realize that you are empty.

Empty.

Even the word itself has a hollow sound. One dear friend of mine described the feeling of emptiness like dropping a stone down a well. However, the well is so deep and so dark, we never hear the splash and we never see the ripples of the stone hitting the water.

The feelings of emptiness that you are experiencing are due to the fact that everything about you comes from other people. You are a child of the collective, rather than a being of your own making. It makes sense to feel this empty when you have used nothing of your true self to build your personality. Yet, there is power and creativity in the emptiness, when you are willing to face the void. When you are willing to dive deep down, you will find your inner treasure, just like the free-diving Ama pearl hunters of Japan.

We have talked in the previous chapter about how we are made up of the expectations that others push on us, and how easy it is to take what they give us and make those things our own thoughts and feelings.

So what happens when you realize how empty you are? The first reaction is usually fear, but after that can come a bright period of real self-discovery, beauty and growth!

Let me show you how to identify that fear, and then to thrive.

Fear in the Darkness

When I think about emptiness, I think about a dark place. I think about being in a deep dark space that has no bounds. Perhaps there is a floor beneath me, but most of the time, I am floating in a black void. I am reaching out for something, but it is only thin air that meets my fingers, and I am groping for something, anything to hold on to!

Of course, it makes sense that the first thing that I find to hold on to is something that I will cling to! It doesn't matter if the thing is sharp, or if it is ugly, or if it is actually trying to hurt me. When you are in the dark and when you are alone and afraid, this is a natural reaction. At least there is something here with you, filling the darkness!

This fear of emptiness is something that feels like we are born with. To survive, we must reach for something more, something to fill that emptiness. If the people around us were loving, positive things were placed in our reach, given to our hands, and we were taught to use them then our life might be a bit easier, smoother.

However, it is far more likely that the things that you found were there because of carelessness or malice. Some things were given to us because our parents were too busy; other things were given to us because the people around us are actively cruel.

For example, let's look at the example of one beautiful woman I know. She was a girl who developed breasts early. When most girls were wearing training bras, she was wearing a C-cup. She was known for her womanly figure, and she began to hate her body in a very real and very scary way.

When she was floating in the darkness, looking for an identity and craving the love and support that we all deserve, she was presented with an idea of her body as overly sexual and a source of embarrassment. This was an idea she latched on to, and as she grew, it turned into a cycle of dressing provocatively and then feeling deeply ashamed of herself for doing so. She had received twin messages saying that her body was meant to attract attention and that it was bad for doing so.

When she spoke of her difficulties in this area, I looked deep in her eyes, and I told her that I wanted her to find her own truth. I wanted her to really look at her body and think about what it was for and how she felt about it.

It was very difficult. At first, it was hard for her to avoid thinking about what her body meant to other people. She kept starting off on things like "Well, men want-" and "Other women think-"

I cut her off four or five times, patiently asking her to come back to what she thought when she thought of her body. Finally, she nodded, and began to speak.

She spoke about how her body shape is inherited from women she loves very much, her grandmother and her mother. She talked about how strong and healthy her body is, and how it carries her where she wants to go. She talked about the extra little bit of fat she carries, and how she secretly likes it because it makes her soft. She talked about how much she liked wearing dresses that allowed her to feel the breeze on her arms and legs.

This is what she should have found in the darkness!

Being Unafraid

When you are in the darkness, I don't want you to be afraid. I know how hard this can be, and I know how much you might be fighting it. After all, you are in an empty place. There's nothing there but you!

Exactly.

That is fully what you need to understand! When you are in an empty place, you still have the very precious and the very valuable thing there that is your self. You are powerful, you are strong, and when you are in an empty place, you don't have to struggle to find someone else to fill it.

Instead, what you have is the opportunity to fill it yourself. You do not need anyone else. When you know who you are and what you are, you will find that it is a wonderful experience to find others to support this, rather than seeking for the approval of others to build yourself up.

Don't be afraid. You are at a wonderful crossroads. You are alone in the emptiness, but you have everything that you need right in front of you. If you are not alone in the emptiness, remove the negative thoughts and road blocks that other people have thrown at you.

There is a reason why these words ring out so true and so compellingly.

"Seek outward, you might find objects of value.
Seek inward, you will find your treasures"

In the last chapter, we spoke about realizing where some old baggage and some old issues come from. When you start getting rid of them, you will feel empty, but now there is the potential for vast growth and change.

Filling the Blank

I want you to focus on one aspect of your life. Ideally, it will be something that you feel conflicted about, or that you even feel negative about. For many people, it is a physical flaw, an issue in their past they cannot get over, or something that troubles them.

I want you to write it down on a piece of paper, and I want you to come at it as if you were an alien. You come from a distant star, and you are curious about everything. You are not a human, so of course you do not understand things like negative stereotypes or preconceptions. Instead, you are looking at everything with fresh eyes.

For example, say that you have written down the fact that you are not very athletic. As a child, it probably made you feel like you were inferior. Perhaps you were teased about it.

11

Now pretend to be that alien.

Oh, this human is a little slower than the others. It does not run as fast, or hit the ball as far. Look at how hard it tries, however! Oh, those other humans are being so cruel to it. What a shame, why would they pick on it for not doing things as fast? These sports are not helping the humans eat or find shelter. Why would anyone be so cruel to someone who cannot do such an inconsequential thing?

An alien would not judge you or think that you were lesser just because you were bad at playing ball as a child. It would be surprised that people would mock you. It would look at what had happened and see something very confusing.

This is a great exercise to show you how little some things really matter. When in doubt, step outside of yourself and look with fresh and compassionate eyes.

Instead of filling yourself with the criticism of others, try filling yourself with compassion and understanding for yourself!

Be generous, and realize that when you create yourself from the nothingness, you can do anything. This emptiness does not define you, nor does the abuse of others.

You design yourself. You create yourself. You are your own creator, just as I am my own creator!

Chapter 3
Letting Go

Your freedom died the day you exchanged
Bliss for pleasure.
- Celina Tio

I once heard a story about a man who was skilled at poker in the era of cowboys and frontiers and cattle drives. This man loved the game, and he had spent years of his life honing the craft of it. Imagine his friend's surprise when he peeked in on this man's game and found him losing terribly!

The friend watched for a moment, and he quickly realized something.

He interrupted the game and drew the skilled poker player outside on a pretext.

"Look, I don't know how you're not seeing it, but you're being cheated! Everyone else at the table is cheating you and taking you for all you are worth."

The skilled poker player nodded, and when his friend didn't look as if he had anything else to say, he started to head back inside.

"Wait, why are you going back to that game? Why would you sit down with people who are cheating you?

"Well, sir, they may be cheating me blind, but it's the only game in town!"

This story has always struck me as a warning about letting go, and what happens if you cannot. This poker player was amazingly good at his game, but the game itself called to him in a way that was detrimental to him.

He loved it so much that he found he could not let go even when he was being cheated and taken for everything he owned.

So what's your poker game? What are you hanging on to?

Letting go of the ideas that other people have about us is hard. Some of these ideas are attractive, some are terrible, and they are all very stubborn, but it needs to be done. Let us show you how.

What Do I Need to Let Go Of?

It can be hard to tell what you need to let go of. Sometimes, holding on to something for a very long time can mean that your grip is locked tight around it. Sometimes, the things that you have hung on to for so long have great meaning to you.

However, simply because you have had it for so long does not mean that it is good for you or even safe for you.

I want you to imagine being a little child again. I want you to think of yourself as small, vulnerable, curious, and completely without fear. Everything in the world is interesting to you, everything is wonderful!

Now I want you to imagine that you have someone looking after you. This person might be a parent, a grandparent, a babysitter or a sibling. There are some of us who are not lucky enough to have had a guiding safe presence in our lives; do your best, and remember that you deserve to be nurtured.

Imagine being a little child and ambling towards the stove. Isn't it pretty? Isn't the ring on the stove red and glowing? Of course you want to touch it!

When you stumble towards the stove, your little hands reaching for it, perhaps your guardian is not looking. It happens to the best of us.

You touch the stove, and oh, it's hot! Your body pulls away quickly in response, almost before your brain realizes what is going on. Your caregiver comes up and tells you that you should not do that, and they run your hand under cold water.

If only everything in life was this easy! In this incident, we learn that fire is hot. It is bad for us, and we are given a clear reason as to why it is bad, and we are given sympathy when we suffered from it. We realize that life is better for us if we do not touch the stove, and we let go of the need to touch the stove right away.

If every negative thing in our life was as clear-cut, it would be simple to move forward in life with absolutely no baggage and no problems at all. We could see the bad things and why they were bad, we would learn before they hurt us too much, and there would be supportive people on hand to tell us why they were bad and to tell us what to do if they happen.

Finding the Negative Things In Your Life

I had a very good friend named June who had another friend that I did not care for at all. I didn't know why I didn't care for

June's friend, but soon enough, I was skipping get-togethers because that person would always be there.

Finally, at a wedding, I saw this friend corner June and just mock her mercilessly for a mistake she had made during the wedding toast. When she left, I walked over to June and right then and there took her aside for a little chat.

"Listen," I said. "That person is not your friend. She is toxic, and you did not deserve that."

To my shock, I saw June's eyes fill up with tears. I hugged her, and she told me that no one had ever told her that that kind of behavior was unacceptable before. She didn't understand that her friend was a negative force in her life.

I was astonished, because it seemed that anyone with common sense would quickly realize what bad news this woman was! How could my smart, sensitive and compassionate friend miss this plain and simple fact?

I met up with June a few days later, and we hashed it out over coffee. I quickly came to realize that this friend came into June's life at a vulnerable time. June had just broken up with a lover, and this woman was there for her.

However, in the years since, the woman had revealed herself to be abusive, abrasive and uncaring.

"So why do you still see her?" I asked, mystified, and June shrugged helplessly.

"I just didn't know she was that bad," June replied. "I didn't know that she was being so terrible to me. I just formed an impression of her as a kind and compassionate person."

Right here, we can see how June managed to be blind to the idea that this woman was bad. Because June's impression of this woman was formed at a sensitive time, she hung on to that.

June needed to let go of that woman, and when she did, many things became much, much better for her.

Are there people or things in your life that you need to get rid of?

We all want to be kind, but when it comes to letting go, you are looking at a kind of growth that needs to happen.

Evaluating Your Life

Here we are. We need to take action, but as you know, letting go of things can be tough. I have friends who cannot let go of so much as a magazine, and I have other friends who remove things with such violent abandon that it feels more like they are cutting pieces off of themselves!

To let things go in a sane fashion that nourishes you, you need practice. It is just like anything else.

I want you to look around you right now, and I want you to pick up the first thing that you lay eyes on. It might be a book, a little knickknack a tool or a piece of computer equipment.

I want you to evaluate its presence in your life. Does it make you happy? Does it serve its purpose? Do you receive delight in some way from it?

If the answer to all of these questions is no, then you need to think about why you have it! Why is it taking up space in your life? Why is it there? Why do you keep it?

Some people keep things for nostalgia, but think about what you are remembering. Are you actually looking at something that is pleasantly nostalgic, or are you simply keeping it because you have always kept it?

Be willing to take a moment to really meditate on what you are looking at. Do you look at it and smile, or do you simply feel kind of dull about it?

I want you to stop and take a deep breath right now. Breathe in, hold the breath, let it out in a long smooth exhale.

Now I want you to say, "The things that bring me love and joy, I will keep. Everything else, I will let go of."

This is the principle that you should apply to your life. Apply it to the people, the things and the activities that you do. Do you find joy in them? Keep them.

Do they bring you nothing of joy or love? Let them go.

This is your journey, and you cannot afford to be weighed down with despair and things that do you no good.

Let it go. Let it go. Let it be. Let it be.

Chapter 4
Discovering Your True Self

My greatest responsibility
Is my own creation,
My own evolution,
My own discovery and celebration of my existence.
- Celina Tio

I love nature, and I feel that if we all spent a small part of each day listening to the world around us, we would come away from the experience lightened and enlightened. We could hear what the world around us was trying to teach us, and we would understand ourselves a lot better than we do now.

I once had a very dear friend who was a firecracker. There was absolutely no better way to put it. He was full of life, full of energy, and he was always running around from one meeting to another. He would be having coffee with me one day and the next he'd be off chasing an employment opportunity across the world. He was an exciting, funny person, but everyone who met him said that he was great in small doses but exhausting in the long run.

I saw something different. I saw someone who was busy for the sake of being busy. One day, to test out my hypothesis, I asked him out for a walk.

I took him to one of the most beautiful green areas in my part of the world, and I walked with him. He chattered about this and that, an award he won, a tumultuous love affair, a possible promotion. I smiled and nodded and listened, but I made sure that I was simply enjoying the day out.

Finally, he ground to a halt, and eyed me with exasperation as I touched the rugged bark of a tree.

"Okay, what's up?" he said. "You've not said anything at all for the last forty minutes. Are you even listening to me?"

I assured him that I was, but I told him that I was also honoring him by letting him be entirely himself, without interruption from me. I wanted him to see who he was without the mirror of other people, and when I said that, he ground to a stop.

"What do you mean?"

"Your true self, the person who exists underneath the clothes, and the travel, and the jobs and the romances, is something that is entirely independent. So many people have this image of you, and when you see it, you try to live up to it. I just wanted to see if I could see what was underneath. I wanted to see the real you."

He paused, and we walked on for a while. He was quiet, far more introspective than I had known him to be. When we got back to my car, he turned to me, and in the most solemn voice I have ever heard out of him, he said the most heartbreaking words I have ever heard:

"I don't know who I am."

Telling the World to Be Quiet

When you think about what you are, a few labels immediately come to mind. You might think of words like "sister," "mother," "lawyer," or "student," and they would not be wrong, but they do not tell the whole story.

You are more than your relationships to other people. You are far more than that, but the world tells us, women especially, that we are only important in so far as we have a relationship with someone else, whether it is a romantic relationship or a familial one.

In the last chapter, we talked about putting aside expectations that are imposed upon us. We thought hard about who other people want us to be, and we realized that letting ourselves be defined by others is not the right path.

Now we must do more work, and the going gets more difficult.

When a child is learning to speak, her mother points at the sky and says "blue." The child is small and does not have language yet. The child looks at the sky, sees the color and repeats after the mother.

The sky is blue because my mother says it is.

However, what would happen if the child was simply asked what color the sky was? A child might glance up on a cloudy day and say "white" or they might look up at a sunset and say "purple" or "pink."

Really understanding yourself is a lot like that. When you are told the sky is blue, you simply repeat it, over and over again without looking up. If someone asks you what color the sky is, you look up, you examine the colors, and you come to your own conclusion about what is going on. This is something that can change the way you think about yourself.

What Color Is Your Sky?

Right now, I want you to do a simple exercise. Read through the simple instructions, and then get started. There are no surprises, but you might startle yourself with what you end up with.

Collect a piece of paper and a pen or pencil, and bring it to the most comfortable place in your home. Ideally it is a place where you will have a little bit of privacy, at a point when people are out of the house or occupied elsewhere.

Sit in a comfortable spot, but not one that is so comfortable that you will fall asleep. Keep the pencil and paper close at hand.

Focus on your breath. Draw your breath steadily in through your nose and exhale out through your mouth. Your breaths need not be deep, but they should be full. Imagine the air traveling through your body, bringing oxygen and life to every part of you.

After a while, when your breathing is slow and natural, I want you to simply be in your body. Draw back from the breathing and let your mind flow where it wants to. Think about yourself. Think about your own soul, a beautiful gleaming thing that lives within your core.

Your soul is something that no one can take away from you. People tell you what's in it all the time, but only you know the truth.

Your soul is you, and at the end of the day, it is untouched and untouchable. Nothing that has happened to you can affect the soul's beauty and power.

Meditate on your soul, on that crystal-pure part of you that is yours and yours alone.

Slowly, open your eyes, and put pen to paper

I am...

Finish the phrase. What are you?

Are you beautiful? You are.

Are you creative and full of life? You are.

Are you unique, one of a kind, a song, a feather, a tree? You are.

You are the only one who defines yourself.

When you are done, take a deep breath, and simply look to see what you have written. In the depths of your own mind, you have always held the secret of who you are and what you are.

Your actions and your outward demeanor might be shaped by the world around you, but if you took all of that away, you would still be who you are without it.

There you are, and you are worthy of the universe!

Empty World

A friend that I love very much, who regularly shares her wisdom with me, once asked me what I would do if all of the people in the world disappeared.

"I'd be very sad that all of my friends and family were gone," I responded gamely, and she nodded.

"Of course you would be," she said practically. "But you need to do something after you stop crying. You need to do something. There you still are, in an empty world, with all of the resources of the planet at your fingertips. What do you do?"

I thought about it, and the answer I came up with surprised my friend not at all. I would gather supplies and I would trek into the woods. I would be surrounded by the trees that have never wondered who they are, and that have never needed to be anything different. I would listen to rivers which don't need to be listened to, to know that they are important, and I would gaze on gorgeous mountain peaks that have never wondered if they were beautiful.

What would you do in an empty world? I realized that I am a child of nature, someone who wants to just be.

Sometimes, our friends and loved ones clue us into aspects of our personality that we never knew existed before, but somewhere, deep down, we know ourselves best.

Think of a beautiful plant that is growing in the garden. Its leaves are lush and green, and it has a beautiful flower growing. However, what if this gorgeous plant has no root? It has nothing to ground itself, nothing to keep it safe or to nourish it.

In this metaphor, the person everyone sees is the plant. It may be beautiful and attractive, but without the root, it is empty and strange. It will never thrive or grow. Instead, it is an illusion, for how could there be a plant without a root?

You need to put down roots, and you need to become a real person, a real thing that does not rely on others. Perhaps that person is not who they expect. Maybe your leaves are a little tattered or your stem is a little thick. Maybe you are strange to them. However, with roots of your own, you will prosper in ways that they never expected, that you never hoped for!

Your true self is a wonderfully perfect thing. I want to meet you. I don't want to see who your friends and family think you are, and I don't want to see who you think you need to be in order to be loved and liked.

I want to see the real you, the worthwhile person that is hiding or buried under all of those labels. I want to know who you are, and I want you to be unafraid.

Come out.

It's time for you to come out, to stretch, and to be who you are. There is no time but now, so embrace your inner self and step out into the light.

Chapter 5
Empowering the Real I

My greatest obligation
Is sharing my creation,
Is sharing my evolution
Celebrating existence
- Celina Tio

Now we are coming to the deepest parts of you. Can you feel it? Can you sense it? Just for a moment, I want you to close your eyes, and I want you to imagine something in your heart, something pushing and pulsing and glowing with life.

There is a deep power inside you, and there is an amazing wellspring of strength too. However, if you have been constrained for all of your born days over the expectations of others, you will quickly come to realize that your inner self might be frail, might be vulnerable!

However, the truth is that inner strength, the real you, the part of you that cries out "I am! I am! I am here and I am ready!" can never be weakened, no matter how long it is put away. Some people find their real inner strength when they are in their teens. Some do not find it until they are in their seventies! Your inner strength is there, and it is waiting to be discovered.

Identifying Your Inner Strength, the Real You

We've talked a great deal about the people who bind us, whether they mean to or not. We have spent a lot of time seeing how people harm us and close us in with their expectations, whether good or bad. If you have spent your whole life being told that you are "the pretty one" maybe you were never encouraged to see how smart and strong you really are!

Sometimes, we want to run from our own strength. What is this heat inside us, we wonder. This feeling... it feels like anger, it is powerful and it is right there! It is so strong, it is so hot and demanding! These things can frighten us very badly if we are not ready for them, but when you feel them, you know you are getting close.

Many people first realize their strength when they are helping others. Think about the mother who will defend her children from anything, or the friend who stands up for those who are treated badly. When these people stand up to bullying, and when they see what is right and wrong and seek to right the wrongs, they are showing off their strength.

It can be shocking to see these people shrink back down once their strength flees, and it is a sad thing as well. Why is it so easy to be strong for others, and so much harder to be strong for yourself? The answer is that we are taught to put our true selves, our true, powerful and beautiful selves away. These selves are too much for the modern world, not gentle enough, not restrained!

The answer, then, is that of course we must nurture our inner selves, the parts of us that are hiding. If we take care of that strength, that strength will take care of us, so follow me along this path to find yourself and your power!

Understanding Care of the Self

What do you need to do when you want to make something strong?

Say that you find a sad little kitten on your way home tomorrow. Poor little thing, it is all scrawny and dirty. You could keep walking by, you could simply leave it behind, but you don't. Instead, you take it home and you feed it. You take it to the veterinarian, and you make sure that it has everything that it needs.

It's a little touch and go for a while. The little kitten is frail, and you worry you might harm it accidentally. However, despite how tiny it is, it is fierce! It grows every day, filling out, getting stronger and becoming more. As you watch, it grows taller and stronger, its coat smooth and sleek because of the food and care you give it.

One day it is a fully grown cat, but it doesn't stop there.

It grows and grows, getting bigger and heavier and fiercer, and you realize one day as it nuzzles your hand and licks your arm with its big raspy tongue that you have brought home a tiger!

Essentially, your strength is that tiger. Neglected all these years, it is small and underfed. Maybe at this point, you can carry it in one hand and hide it with another. Maybe it has even been starved or abused. Things happen sometimes.

However, it is still there, and you have the ability to find it and to nurture it. When you feed it, it will grow, and before you know it, it will grow into something that will protect you, care for you. It will become more obvious and more visible, and soon other people will see your true self and your sense of power!

In this analogy, it is very easy to see what the kitten needs. A kitten meows for food, and when it wants to play, it climbs all over you and demands your attention. It can be a little harder to look at your own inner strength and see what is required there, but it is far from impossible.

Everything that we value needs love and care, so now you need to think about how to acquire it.

Self Care

Right now, I want you to take five dollars from your wallet or to deduct five dollars mentally from a credit or debit card. Five dollars is a small amount of money for many, but its buying power creates a sufficient impact. If you use that five dollars, chances are good that your finances will be just fine! However, that five dollars is really a ticket to taking care of yourself.

I want you to take that five dollars and I want you to use it for something that will bring you delight. I do not care what it is; if you can bring yourself some joy with five dollars, I want you to do it!

Some people will drop that money into a needy person's hand, and that is fine. They live to delight others, and this is a way that they can do so.

Other people will go and buy a tube of lipstick, and that is fine as well. They are bringing beauty into their own lives and a dash of color to their world.

Still others will purchase a new paint color or a box of crayons, something that they can use to create art, and that is wonderful. They are bringing a little of the beauty that makes them up into the real world.

Others will simply purchase a drink from their favorite coffee shop, whether it is something with bitter tea or sweet caramel in it, and this is lovely. They are feeding their body, and they are giving themselves comfort.

When you want to nurture your inner strength, the first thing that you need to do is to take care of yourself. Your strength and your real self are going to be in hiding until they get the help and the care that they need, and it is up to you to make sure that they know they are wanted.

When you take care of yourself, you are nurturing yourself and loving yourself. This is not a skill that we are taught when we are young. We are told to believe that we should always keep the best for other people, and that we should always think about those less fortunate.

I will tell you a secret, however; one that I had to learn through a great deal of living and joy and pain.

If you cannot take care of yourself, you cannot take care of anyone!

Think about that greatness and that strength inside yourself. If you nourish and feed it, you can reach out to others. You can help them find their strength just as you have found yours. When you feed and nurture your strength, you are creating a world where something wonderful can happen. There has never been a bad time to become strong. It is never too soon or too late.

When you decide to nourish and to love your own strength, you are finding your own self, and your own self is not a weak kitten. It is a tiger, and you just have to help it and love it and feed it up. Take care of yourself.

Only you know what you need, and only you can truly take care of yourself. Pay attention to what your soul is crying out for, and be willing to reach out and to embrace that need. Give it the same attention and love that you would to a crying kitten, and soon enough, you will see yourself bloom.

This is something that can change the world for you. Find your "I." Find your inner strength and your real self, and then take good care of it!

Chapter 6
Body, Mind and Spirit

Unique, pure, vibrant ... that is my seed.
- Celina Tio

We so often think of ourselves as a patchwork of different parts and pieces. It's as if the mind wants one thing, but the body needs another. The body may need rest but the mind insists on continuing. The spirit may want quiet but the ego is afraid of loneliness. The truth is that all of these parts are one, and to bring them into harmony, you must know how to listen.

We talked in the last chapter about the fact that you simply must take care of yourself, and the honest truth is that of course you deserve it! You are a special and strong person, and you deserve care. You deserve the best, and not just the outside of you, either! In this chapter, we address your body, your mind and your spirit.

Some people see these three parts as being at war with one another. The body wants one thing, the mind wants another, and the spirit is on an entirely different plane. The truth is that all three are crying out for the same thing. They want to be healthy, and they want to be whole!

It is only humans that persist in seeing themselves and each other in parts, but the truth of the matter is that only when you see yourself as a whole can you make progress. The only issue is that these things all need to be approached in a specific way.

How can you bring your body, your mind and your spirit into harmony? How can you use them to become stronger, and to become a truer, more complete you?

Let us take this journey one step at a time and move towards a stronger you together.

Your Body, Your Vehicle

Your body is the one thing you will have with you for your entire life, and isn't it a shame that you spend so much time disliking it? The unfortunate thing is that many people get caught up in what their bodies can't do, and they forget to look at what they can do. This is something that can be quite shocking and troubling in the long run.

After all, your body is yours. It is a part of you, the part that allows you to see, to feel, to taste and to hear. It is the way that you interact with the world, and as such, it deserves love and respect!

When you want to take good care of your body, start listening to it. Lie very still and think about what it is telling you. Is it sore? Is it stiff? Is it hungry? Because we spend so much time wandering through life being told to do this or not to do that, we end up ignoring our bodies a lot. We do not respect them, and we do not pay attention until they are screaming for us.

Gather up a hand towel and a bit of coconut or jojoba oil, and go to your bathroom sink. Toss the towel into the sink and run hot water over it. As you do so, take the oil in your hand and massage it into your face. If you have long hair, it will be a good thing to tie it back first. Be loving, and rub your face with care. You are massaging love and life into your soft skin, and you are pampering yourself.

When the oil is well rubbed into your skin, take the wet hot cloth and wring it out. Be careful, as it is likely very hot at this point! Lay it over your face, and leave it there for one minute. After you are done, use the cloth to wipe the rest of the oil off of your skin. It is important that you get the oil off as thoroughly as possible.

When you are done, you will find that your skin glows. It has been cleansed and loved, and it will show you how wonderful those things are. This exercise only took a few minutes. Now imagine that wellness and sense of peace spreading through the rest of your body!

Remember that your body should feel good. It is a part of you. It is not a trap, it is not flawed. Instead, it is perfect, so take care of it. It is something you should treasure.

Your Mind, Your Pilot

If your body is a vehicle, your mind is your pilot. It is the thing that takes charge, that thinks fast and that helps you interact with the complicated people around you. Your mind is like a knife, sharp and beautiful, and if you treat it poorly, you can get cut just as badly!

When you want to take care of your mind, you need to feed it. Your mind needs nourishment just like your body does. However, the things that you feed your mind are new things. Every brain feeds on novelty. Minds want to be challenged, and they want to feel the satisfaction of having done a good job, something to be proud of.

One of the best things you can do for your brain is to learn. When your brain learns, it is in the most active state that it can be. Remember that learning is something that will keep you young and inquisitive no matter how old you are, and it is something that will always be a benefit to you.

It matters less what you learn than the spirit with which you learn it. For example, think about math. Lots of people have problems with math, and whenever they think about it, they make an angry face. However, the problem with math is usually the way that it is taught, not the subject itself!

If you are willing to be slow and patient with yourself, and if you are in a good place, your brain can take you on some of the most wondrous adventures you have ever been on. Life is wonderful, and there is an endless assortment of things to learn, of things to do and to feel and explore.

Consider some of these ways to nourish your mind:

*Learn a new language

*Paint a picture

*Sing a song that you have just learned

*Take a class at your local learning establishment

*Write a poem

*Tell a story

*Learn to cook something entirely new

There are so many wonderful things for you to learn that this list could be endless. Think about the thing that you have always wanted to do, and do it. There are no limits to what your mind can do, so allow yourself to learn. Allow yourself to be bad at things at first and to have some fun with new things. There is no harm at all in trying something new, even if you don't stick with it.

Utilize your mind in a positive way. Let go of resentment, hurt, fear, pain, sadness, anger, jealousy. Those of my clients who consciously go through this process find themselves freer, more relaxed and more optimistic and confident of their futures.

These are some of the comments that I get:

"I find I have more time during the day."

"I find it hard to get upset."

"I can concentrate more on what I'm doing."

"I enjoy things more, my mind is clear and I'm able to think more positively."

To these responses, I always say "Excellent! Now is the time for you to live your life as you intend it. You are now truly the creator of your life's experiences."

Be ready to let your mind lead you on some of the most fantastic adventures you could ever go on!

Your Spirit, Your Compass

Though the desires of the mind and body are often clear enough, finding and understanding the desires your spirit may seem, to many, to be more complex. Yet, it's the simplest thing you can do, to get in touch with your spirit, and that is by slowing down to listen. To me, the spirit is the same as the soul, and I shall use the words interchangeably.

When you want to encounter your spirit, start by sitting still, quiet and comfortable. Imagine yourself walking down a long hall full of light. You are suffused with a sense of wellness and with peace. Along either side of the hall, to your left and your right, are doors.

There are many kinds of doors. Some of them are made of wood, some are just a drape of fabric, others are steel security doors. You know that no matter how imposing they look or how tough they seem, they will open for you. It does not trouble you.

You keep walking until you find a door that feels right. Maybe it is a door out of a fantasy novel, with black iron bands, or maybe it is the door of the house you grew up in.

Yes, this is the right one, you think. This is the one I need.

You open the door.

What do you find inside?

Some people only find a feeling, something soft and wonderfully loving and vulnerable. Other people see an object, while still others see a person. Maybe that person looks like them, or maybe it is someone they have never met before.

That is your spirit.

Once you know it, you are ready to begin. You are ready to help it grow, to expand and to become beautiful, and that is a wonderful thing!

Your spirit or soul is the spark of light that came into this world in physical form. But your spirit also resides in a different dimension - it is a wonderful, vibrant being that is always waiting for us to connect to. It is the voice that tells you to sing your song, to create your art, to reach out for your dreams. Your soul is part of the creation of the Universe and there is absolutely nothing that the Creator has manifested that is not significant. You are a part of creation, you are made from the same energy and materials as are far-flung stars and galaxies. You are powerful.

As you can tell, the thing that all of these exercises have in common is that they are getting you ready for action! They are preparing your mind, body and soul for helping you get what you want, for realizing your real you.

There is a whole world out there of people to meet and things to experience, and if you want to go there joyfully, you need to venture out as a whole person. This is an important thing for you to realize. There is no part of you that is less worthy or less beautiful. Our worst nightmare should be not to live our dreams; that is what I say and believe.

All of you are wonderful. All of you are worthy!

Embrace your wholeness and now venture forth!

Chapter 7
Harness Your True Power

From this moment on,
I live knowing that I AM
and passionate about becoming all that I dream my life to be.
- Celina Tio

What comes to mind when you think of power? Do you visualize brawny muscle-builder, who uses his physical strength to boss others around? Do you a picture a ruler or king who wields the power of life and death over another? Do you imagine sizzling electricity conjuring light and energy??

While all of these things are true to some extent, I want to offer you a different solution.

Stand before a mirror, and take a long and close look at yourself. See with judgement who you are, without the words and phrases and expectations of others clouding your mind. Look and know that the person in the mirror is the one person who has gotten you this far, to this exact point in your life.

You have undergone difficult experiences that may have broken others. You have achieved victories that you are proud of, and you have committed mistakes that you are not proud of. You have created a home within yourself, and every day, you prove your strength.

When you want an image of power in front of you, look in a mirror! That is all that you have do; that is all that you ever have to do.

You have a power that has gotten you this far; now you need to harness it even more to move firmly and resolutely in the direction of your dreams. This power has served you well, and now I shall show you how to make it serve you even better.

I Have A Right to Be Here

Think about the way a mouse enters a room. It skulks to the side of the door, it clings to the wall. Every few minutes, it stops to sniff the air for tell-tale smells of a predator, or for threats to its existence. A mouse hurries out to the middle of the floor to grab a few crumbs that it needs to live, and then it scurries back to the wall before heading right for the door.

Now think about the way that a cat enters the room, particularly a cat that knows exactly where it is and what it wants. It strides into the room, glancing left and right to see what is going on. It ignores the people that it dislikes, and it heads right for the people that it cares for. It headbutts you for affection, it demands to be fed, and whether it is happy or angry, the whole world knows it!

How do you enter the room? I have known too many dear friends who enter the room like mice, and I will tell you exactly why they do that. They think that, like the mouse, they have no right to be where they are. They feel as if they are unwelcome, that they have to take the crumbs that they can get, and that once they have those crumbs, they should make themselves scarce and let the cats take the scene!

Many of my friends and I enter the room like cats. We look around to see what's up, we skip the people we don't care for, and we head right for the people who we know are going to delight us! We know beyond a shadow of a doubt that we are here to be ourselves and no one else, and if you have always thought of yourself as a mouse, you know that that is power!

Power starts from you. You are powerful, and when you want to harness that inner power, you need to think about how you can move towards a special kind of awareness of yourself. You need to be able to reach out and be someone who is taken seriously, who is liked and respected and worth talking to.

Start by channeling a cat. Every cat knows that it is exactly where it needs to be. Every cat is aware of how important it is in the grand scheme of the universe.

When you enter a room, remember that people do not look on you as they would look on a mouse. You are a person, you have the rights that everyone else has, and if someone tries to deny you those rights, they are a bully and they are not worth your time!

Enter the room as a cat does, aware of your own worth and your own importance. You don't have to earn other people's regard; they have to earn yours!

Writing Up a Storm

I am a writer. I look at words and I see worlds in them. When you write to me, I can see what kind of person you are, and I can see how you want to present yourself. Words are important, whether you are speaking them or writing them down, but when you look at the written word, some patterns become clear.

I want you to take a look at the last few texts and emails that you sent. When you need something to be done, are you asking them about it, or are you telling them that things need to be done? Most of us were raised to ask, but the world needs us to tell.

For example, say that you are writing to your bank to talk about an error on their part. Which of these lines sounds like something that you would write?

"Whenever you get a moment, could you please look into this error?"

"Please correct this error at once, and return the money to my account."

When you ask, you are giving the other person all of the power. When you tell them what is going to happen, you are keeping the power yourself and giving them the need to please you and to make things right.

If you are someone who is more inclined to write the top line, take a close look at the second line. There is nothing impolite about it, nor is there anything offensive about it. It will get the job done much faster, and it is a great way to assert yourself.

Real power can start with your voice and with your words. Do not allow yourself to get derailed by pleasantries and by questioning your own authority and your own needs. Make your needs known, use please and thank you, and remember that simply being polite does not require you to be a push over. This is something that can make you go from shy to powerful!

Stand Tall

Have you ever heard the saying that the mind is the plaything of the body? It's true! There is a biofeedback loop between your brain and your body. Usually we think of having a feeling and then having a physical response to follow it. For example, when you are happy, you smile.

However, when you are down and you need a pick me up, remember that smiling can make you feel happy. Give it a shot the next time you are feeling down!

One way to take advantage of this biofeedback loop is to stand tall. Stand up straight, throw your shoulders back, and plant your fists on your hips. Make sure that your feet are at least shoulders' width apart, and throw back your head so that you are looking a little higher than you are used to.

Move into this pose and feel the way that power courses through you. This is the pose of heroes and people who know what they want, and it is an intoxicating way to really assert yourself. You have a power that lies in your bones and your DNA, and it is a natural part of you and what you offer to the world.

Try this pose whenever you have a quiet moment. If you are getting ready to do something big and important, simply strike the pose in private before you head out to do your thing. Realigning your energy this way makes a big difference to your chances for success.

If you need to access this power in a more subtle way, simply straighten your spine, push your shoulders back and raise your chin a touch. Holding yourself this way is a subtle way of commanding respect. It is a good way to remind yourself of how strong you really are.

Are you ready to be as powerful as you want to be? Are you ready to take advantage of what you have inside? You have spent far too long simply being bound by the power that others were willing to give you. Now you can take it for yourself!

You are powerful, and anyone who tells you otherwise is not your friend. Leave behind your doubts and your fears, and embrace something wonderful and perfect instead.

This is something that can change the way you live your life, so give up your weakness and choose power.

Chapter 8
Change Is Evolution

We are witnessing creation as we are included in creation.
Our creation is included in the expansion of the universe.
- Celina Tio

Some people state that there is no meeting between science and spirituality, and to those people, no matter which side of the argument they are on, I say "You are just not creative enough!" The wedding of science and spirituality takes us higher in our understanding of the world around us. There are things that neither science nor spirituality can explain, and there are wonderful things that both speak of with passion.

Ever since I was young, I loved the idea of evolution. Over a period of time that might stretch for eons, we learn more and more about who we are meant to be. Animals change shape, take on new forms. Plants become strange and beautiful, amazingly specialized to their niche in the world.

Evolution gives us a wonderful place to look at our own growth, to realize that becoming the real versions of ourselves is inevitable, and to realize, once and for all, that we are very much a part of the world that we live in.

Understanding Evolution

The first thing we must understand when we are looking at a real change of the self is what evolution is. At the most basic level, it is a change from being one thing to being another. This is the process that leads to animals first leaving the primordial seas, to seeking a way to climb the tall ferns and to finally launching themselves into the sky.

However, the first thing that you must understand about this process and how it relates to you is that it is slow. When you look at the science of it, it is unlikely that you will see even the tiniest fraction of the change of a real species in a lifetime. Similarly, the evolution of the self is also slow, although not the way it is for scientific evolution!

As humans, we want the comfort of consistency. We always want to keep things the same, and we are always invested in making sure that we have the comfort that we need to feel safe. As it turns out, a lot of the things that promote evolution and good change are painful, or at least uncomfortable.

However, going from the sea to the land was hard, as was the process of birds gaining wings that they could use to fly.

We cannot live our lives in complacency and comfort. No matter who you are or what you are doing, it is important to remember that pain will occur, but instead of shying away from it, remember that it is something that will turn you into a more enhanced, more beautiful, more amazing version of yourself!

When evolution comes knocking at your door, you may at first think that it is something terrible, even if your heart quickens a little. Change is coming, and as we grow, we start to evolve and we transform.

Change Is Slow

When people think of change, they typically think of something that is quite fast. Poets like to talk about how things can change in the blink of an eye, and although this is true, the change that occurs inside you, that helps you to mature and to move forward and to be truly yourself, is something that takes much longer.

It is not a matter of looking up and saying that you will always be brave and strong and uniquely yourself from now on. That is something that the movies and the books give us, and while it makes for good cinema, it is simply not true. That may very well be where change begins, but it also needs to progress for a long time.

It starts with little things, and they are quite difficult at first. A long time ago, one of my dearest friends decided that she needed to have better boundaries with her sister. She started saying no to her, which was very difficult at first. It took her a great deal of time and a great deal of courage, and sometimes, she still gave in to things that she didn't want to do because she was tired or simply lacked the resources to resist.

However, she persisted, and over the course of a year, she got better and better about the boundaries that were meant to keep her happy and safe. One day, her sister made a request that she did not like, and she simply said no without thinking about it.

My friend was shocked afterward. She had gone from being someone who would drop anything for a toxic relationship with her sister, and now she could say no without thinking twice about it and go on to enjoy a very good day on her own.

This change did not occur overnight, and it was not an easy process. As you can see, it also did not move in a straight line. There were stops and starts, and days when it was just too tiring. At the end of it all, though, change was inevitable, and my friend grew into a more independent person with better boundaries.

Direct Your Own Evolution

When people look at evolution, they often see something that needs to be driven by fear or pain. This is not the case. Sometimes, though, we can evolve simply because we want to. We see something in our lives that tells us, now it is time to change, and we can follow it.

For example, think of a part of yourself that makes you unhappy. Maybe you are too shy when you go out and you end up missing opportunities that you would like to take part in. Maybe you are guilty of speaking over people that you care about and being too loud and too angry when you do speak. There are plenty of different traits that may be taking you away from your bliss, and no matter what it is, it is something that you can change.

Think about all of the time that you spend feeling bad about a certain topic, and instead, now think about all of the fun that you could have if you channeled that energy towards something much more productive.

Start watching yourself, and start thinking about how you can change yourself. This is what it takes to become the real version of yourself, the wonderful one that is waiting to become.

Embrace Yourself at Every Step!

People speak a lot about forgiving yourself for the mistakes you will make along the way. Instead of forgiving yourself, I want you to stop and really love yourself! Mistakes and false starts are all a part of the evolution process, and if you let them stop you, you will never get to where you are meant to go. This does not mean that you should revel in your mistakes. Instead it means that you should take them as they are meant, which is as signs of progress. If you do everything effortlessly, it would mean that you are simply not doing something very difficult at all.

Embrace yourself as you change, love yourself while you change, and be patient with yourself as you change. You must always take care of yourself, and your time of evolution is no different!

Learning to Love Change

Of course one of the great things that we must understand is that change is frightening. As the caterpillar weaves its snug cocoon to become a beautiful butterfly, one imagines that it is protesting the entire time.

"No," it must think. "How can I be other than what I am? What will become of me? Will I still be me, and will I still matter?"

However, the caterpillar knows exactly what needs to be done, and even if it protests, it will do it anyway. There are no other options when you want to progress to the next stage of yourself, and even if things are frightening, you must take that step forward.

When you feel yourself change, a certain amount of fear and doubt is natural. Wise people recognize this fear and doubt for what they are and do not allow these things to stop them. When you feel a change coming on, take a moment and consider how you can move forward towards your own destiny.

Let that fear and doubt drive you forward instead of forcing you back, and learn to love them for what they are, which is to say, agents of change. They are the trappings of the coming of something much greater, and they can make a huge difference to the way that you turn out.

Do not allow yourself to be stopped by fear. Learn to love the changes that are overtaking you, and learn to direct them. Change is going to happen whether you want it to or not, and so you must learn to love it for the beneficial thing it is.

Chapter 9
Obtaining Real Long-Term Happiness

When we do what we truly love, we bring creation into existence.
- Celina Tio

If you were to ask people what they wanted, what they truly, deep in their hearts wanted for their lives, you would get a lot of different answers. One person would say that they wanted to be free to travel, another person might say that all they wanted was a snug home for their family. Other people are more extravagant, stating that they want careers in the movies or perhaps they love the idea of a real jet-setting lifestyle.

When you get right down to it, however, everyone wants the same thing. No matter what path we take to get there, we want to be happy!

When I look at my life, I see something that suffuses me with a warm glow of satisfaction. I see a wonderful set of people who I love and who love me, I see a home that I have made my own, and I see a life that has succeeded not because of my circumstances but because of me.

Does that mean my life is perfect?

No, absolutely not! Everyone has problems, and everyone gets frustrated. I get angry about things, sad about others, but at the bottom of it, there is the knowledge that I am exactly where I am supposed to be. I have created a happy place for myself, and if I am saying anything with this book, I am saying that!

Finally, here we are at the end of this journey together. I love endings in some ways because they are always the beginning of something new. When one thing ends, something new begins, and as I send you out on your own or if you have decided to do so, to continue further in your journey with me, towards goals I can give you, I leave you with a few thoughts.

Happiness Is Personal

Remember that my happiness is not your happiness. The happiness of celebrities on television is not your happiness. The happiness enjoyed by your family and your friends is not necessarily your happiness.

What makes you happy are not the same as the things that will make other people happy and vice versa. As long as your happiness is not hurting someone, you have the right to pursue it with fervor and determination. As far as we know, we get one ride on this wonderful world, and it would be a shame to spend your days chasing someone else's happiness.

I once knew a man who had it all.. He was handsome, wealthy, well-educated and charming. However, at the end of the day, he was miserable! He was self-medicating with alcohol, and what I helped him to realize was that he was going down the path that his own father had gone down before him.

"Did it make your father happy?" I asked him one day, and he paused.

"I don't know..."

"Well, how did he act? Did he look happy or content?"

"Oh god no," the man responded. "He was always angry, always bitter. He couldn't deal with anything being the least bit out of place, and he would complain about not really having a family when he was on his way out the door to work another 60 hour week!"

He paused and he said very quietly, "The way that I do."

We talked about it, and we realized that his father was chasing a happiness that wasn't his. Perhaps he was ordered to chase it by his own father, or perhaps somewhere along the line, he lost track of what really makes someone happy.

"Either way," I said decisively, "this does not have to be the happiness that you chase."

One of the great advantages that this man had, aside from his natural charm and the wealth he had accumulated, was the ability to make decisions fast and to make them stick.

In the space of six months, he had given up his share in his business, reconciled with his wife and very young child, and moved all three to a hobby farm. He didn't know much about farming, but he did have faith in his ability to learn. Within a year, his family was raising alpacas and chickens, growing their own food and were happier than they ever had been.

From a big city businessman to an eco-conscious farmer might sound like a big leap, but it was simply the distance his heart had to travel to find happiness.

Do You Listen to Your Heart?

We've talked so much about the collectively created self and the person that the people around us want us to be. The truth underneath it all is that we know what makes us happy. We have known this since the time we were small. The problem is that society and the people around us, some of them loving, some of them not, find themselves throwing sand on top of it.

In the midst of the tumult, it is very hard to listen to our hearts. It is very difficult to find out who we are underneath it all.

Now you need to get some practice determining what your happiness is and what you want out of it. You must listen to your heart!

Sit and meditate for a while in a quiet place. You may do this first thing in the morning when your thoughts are fresh and clear, or you might choose to do this late in the evening, when the day's work is done.

Sit and clear your mind. Do not let anything touch you, free yourself to fly above your body. Feel compassion and love for yourself. You have roles that you take on that are important, but they are roles. They are not what you are. You are you. You are unique and special in all the universe, and throughout the world, there is no one else like you.

No one can do things the way that you do, and no one can see things as lovingly and as carefully as you do.

When you see yourself like this, and when you are capable of beholding everything that you are, things get much more simple.

There is a beat in your heart, and if you listen to it, it has words. What does the beat of your heart tell you? What command is written deep inside you?

Is it "I love my family?" Is it "I want to see the world?" Is it "I want to help others?" Is it "I want to be in nature?" Is it "I want to create art?"

The happiness that is inside you might startle you. It might run counter to everything that you have ever been told or it might fly in the face of what you always have tried to do.

The truth of the matter is that happiness is not for people who are emotionally weak. Being happy takes guts, courage and energy. Some people look at their happiness and they feel sick. They feel worried and scared, and they turn away from it.

Do it again.

Your happiness may startle you or even make you feel bad. Sit and meditate again. See what kind of answers you get as you think about it. As you do this over and over again, your path to happiness becomes clear.

Happiness is easier for some people than it is for other people, and after all, the universe is not always as kind as we want it to be. However, what I believe and what all happy people believe is that you can always be happier than where you are.

Your happiness is not always easy. Sometimes, it takes years of work or study or searching. However, happiness is not a zero-sum game. You will not work towards a goal, being unhappy or bland the whole time, achieve it, and suddenly become happy.

Instead, happiness is something that you accumulate. It is something that builds up around you as you get closer and closer to your true self. As you take steps towards your dreams, happiness will come to you, and this is something I and the universe guarantee!

Be Well

Perhaps this is where we will part ways, or perhaps this is where you decide to follow me to a deeper happiness.

No matter what you do, have confidence in yourself and faith in the person you are. You are more than someone's child or someone's parent. You are more than what you do to survive or to make money. You are more than your body, and you are more than the things you make.

You are a human being, whole, beautiful and perfect. You are capable of great things, and when you are happy, you glow with a light that is perfectly your own.

Be someone who is happy.

Make that decision right now, and you will see the fruits of it sooner rather than later. Happiness is something you can attain, so do not put it off tomorrow or leave it off until "later."

Chapter 10
Claim Your Freedom

Going from worthless to priceless only takes deep appreciation
- Celina Tio

My name is Alejandra Logrono; this is my story about how working with Celina changed my life. I was seeking help to deal with all the stuff I was going through. There was a lot going on in my life. I felt stuck with no motivation, low self-esteem, and low self-confidence. I finally decided to get started in the transition to become a better person. It's been a long process leaving the past behind and starting a new life with new goals, high expectations and dreams. Many are still to be accomplished but most important of all is learning to love myself. I'm a new person; at times I don't recognize who I am. I know I still have a long way to go but the changes I have undergone have been empowering. I'm glad that I made the decision to get to know myself. Now I treasure who I am. I am living a new beginning and I'm starting a very successful life as my true self.

That is a testimonial from one of my clients, who has willingly given me permission to share her story. For having had the courage to consciously make a change, Alejandra is now happier, more comfortable in her own skin and is now daring to hitch her wagon to the stars, when once she hung her head down in frustration and unhappiness.

Much more succinct but just as eloquent is this testimonial from Elias Molina.

Thank you Celina for guiding me into my most forgotten part of life, ME!!!

The third testimonial is offered by Sandra Cordero, Co-Founder of the Coalition For Mental Health Toronto, ON. Canada.

It was approaching the 4th anniversary of my brother's passing of an apparently intentional overdose. His sudden death left me bereft with unanswered questions and sadness. In my car, I was listening to the radio program Voces Latinas, hosted by Martha Pinzon on 1610 AM when Celina came on the air to talk about her work in helping people find their inner selves, to let go of the past, to find inner peace and embrace this beautiful life.

She recounted her own life experiences and how she came to recognize the inner love, strength and potential that rest in all of us. She explained on the radio interview, that one day she gave herself a choice. She said, "I could live resenting life or I could fall in love with life and embrace it fully." That was the beginning of her own healing.

She went on to talk about the power and tools to be found in our mind, soul and spirit and how she guides her clients into their own healing and self-discovery.

That interview encouraged me to take back my life. Although I was no longer feeling the profound sadness I had immediately after my brother's death, there was something stopping me from feeling peaceful and whole. So I called Celina and made an appointment.

She helped me comprehend that there was so much, childhood memories, the passing of my siblings and my mother, specially the unanswered questions around my brother's suicide, failed relationships... I had been on a tough road for a long while.

The day of my appointment came. I wasn't sure how it was going to go but I got ready and went to meet Celina.

I arrived at her office and encountered a lovely and professional person. I quickly felt that she genuinely cared to help me, and listened attentively. When I finished she explained how we were going to work together for the following weeks, and we started.

Those sessions are fundamental to how I feel about my life today. I feel happy and whole. Celina helped me comprehend that I was carrying around with me a lot of unacknowledged baggage. Through my work with her, I came around to connecting to the love that my mother always had for me. I then found it within me to forgive her in my heart despite her mistakes.

Feeling stronger inside allowed me to let go of my siblings who have passed on. Paradoxically, by letting go, I felt more fully their love for me. I know now they are always with me.

It was more difficult for me to let go of the brother who took his own life. I remember at his passing I said, "A part of him lives with me and a part of me left with him."

In my sessions with her, Celina encouraged me to give back the part of my brother that I was holding on to and to take back the part of me that I had given to him so that he could peacefully move on into the light. I initially resisted the idea and was not immediately capable of relinquishing the tie. Celina respected my answer and continued with the session.

However, she had planted a seed in me and after the session, I understood that I was not going to feel better if I didn't say good bye.

The months have gone by. I feel free of past unhappy memories, free of those feelings that previously robbed me of inner peace. Even though I could not say good bye to my brother when first prompted by Celina, that didn't stop the natural healing that was happening inside me.

Today, I have the determination and self-control to succeed and live my life fully.

Celina ensured that I didn't get lost in the past. She guided me back to True North and I am now a positive woman, humbled by the blessings of having much love to give and much love to receive. I am open to sharing my life with positive, loving, healthy people.

I now have a new sense of purpose and I'm full of constructive ideas for projects to help out my community.

I sometimes miss my sessions with Celina because I enjoyed them so much. From time to time I call her to say hello.

Celina is the key driver that guides you to claiming your inner treasures and using your inner beauty in your daily life.

Now I know my power, I know my greatness, I embrace my life and above all, I love my self!

Uncovering Your Blessed, Inner Self

Do you feel you are walking as if life has put all its weight on you, a burden so heavy you can't move forward?

If you are feeling depressed and disconnected, how can you regain your joy of living?

If you are hurting because you've been hurt, how do you learn to trust again? If you are in pain because you've lost someone you dearly love, how can you open your heart again?

The answer lies in right here, inside you. You don't have to travel thousands of miles to find your solace and your faith and your comfort, you only need to travel within. If I can sit down to talk to you, I would love to do so to help you connect directly with your inner being. Your inner being, your inner self is the little voice that is speaking to you to let you know that you are misaligned with your true self.

If you are hurt and depressed, your inner being is wanting you to discover your true essence.

If you are hurting because others were mean to you, your inner being is wanting you to know that you are kind.

If you've lost someone, perhaps your inner being wants you to know that you've love within you to give to others.

Your true self wants you to be grateful that you had a wonderful being with you who helped you grow for a period of time. Maybe the lesson is to come around to fully appreciating your own light and the lights of those who are around you, rather than depreciating your own value or feeling less than.

You may now be in great pain but if you are willing to move through the aches, the discomfort and the grief, there are great gifts waiting for you.

Imagine drops of rain falling into a river. Is a single drop less worthy than the mighty river? If the river could speak, it would say that each drop contributes to its flow.

We are all special and valuable. You are special and valuable. In bringing this book to a close, I would like you to think about this.

Your heart beats at the same frequency as the rhythm of our planet, as does mine. Our planet beats in tune with the Universe. It must, otherwise life can't survive. Therefore, our hearts, yours and mine, beat at the same frequency as the Universe. As you create, as you evolve, you are contributing to the expansion of the Universe. That's how valuable you are.

To discover and honor your unique inner treasures through my program Honor Your Inner Treasures™ contact me at: info@honoryourinnertreasures.com.

Appendix

It takes only a single step to move from feeling worthless to feeling priceless. On this page, I invite you to write the simplest things in your life or even in the space where you are right now that you find treasured and precious. It can be as simple as "I love the way the sun shines through the windows onto my plants" or "I treasure this cup of coffee – it warms me up!" You can appreciate anything, anyone, any sense or smell or touch.

Start each sentence with
"I deeply appreciate………."

I further invite you fill this blank page with as many notes of appreciation as you can think of at this moment. Alternatively, you may write one or two lines now and return to this page at another time. I thank you for having come on this journey with me.

Free Bonuses go to:
www.HonorYourInnerTreasures.com